Lincoln Christian College

W9-CAE-264

# EVANGELISM—

## COMMITMENT AND INVOLVEMENT

*Jesse Moren Bader*
1886-1963

# EVANGELISM—

## Commitment and Involvement

### "GOD . . . RECONCILING THE WORLD"

*The N.E.A. Lectures on Evangelism for 1964*

Edited by J. Edward Moseley

THE BETHANY PRESS ⟡ St. Louis, Missouri

*Copyright* © *1965 by The Bethany Press*

Library of Congress Catalog Card Number 65-18203

Scripture quotations, unless otherwise noted, are from the *Revised Standard Version of the* Bible, copyrighted 1946 and 1952 by the Division of Christian Education, National Council of Churches of Christ in the United States of America and used by permission.

Distributed by Thomas C. Lothian, Melbourne, Australia, and Auckland, New Zealand and by The G. R. Welch Company, Toronto, Canada

MANUFACTURED IN THE UNITED STATES OF AMERICA

269
M89

DCHS
NASHVILLE

740

8 MAR 71

38701

DEDICATED

To the memory of
JESSE M. BADER

## Officers and Directors, 1964-66

### NATIONAL EVANGELISTIC ASSOCIATION
#### OF THE
### CHRISTIAN CHURCH (DISCIPLES OF CHRIST)

Dyre Campbell, PRESIDENT
James Clayton Pippin, VICE-PRESIDENT
Donald M. Salmon, GENERAL SECRETARY
Mrs. Arlene Dux Rothenburger, CORRESPONDING SECRETARY
George I. Myers, TREASURER

*Terms Expiring in 1966*

| | |
|---|---|
| Carlton C. Buck | Newell M. Hall |
| James Lee Christensen | Ralph W. Pollock |
| Paul C. Duncan | William A. Sessions, Jr. |

Charles H. Webb

*Terms Expiring in 1967*

| | |
|---|---|
| Ting Rodney Champie | James R. Lewis |
| Harold W. Deitch | James Clayton Pippin |
| Forrest D. Haggard | Richard L. Saunders |

Norman R. Stacey

*Terms Expiring in 1968*

| | |
|---|---|
| Spencer M. Adamson* | Thomas J. Gibbs, Jr. |
| Hubert L. Barnett | Daniel E. Huff |
| Paul M. Bolman | Laurence V. Kirkpatrick |

Frank Edmund See

*Ex-Officio*
J. Daniel Joyce

---

*Deceased.

6

# Contents

# Foreword

THIS VOLUME OF LECTURES IS dedicated to the memory of Jesse Moren Bader (1886-1963). He was known as "Mr. Evangelism" in the fellowship of the Christian Church (Disciples of Christ), of which he was a minister and member, and throughout the ecumenical forces in America and the rest of the English-speaking world.

The decision to publish this book arose in the executive committee of the National Evangelistic Association. This is an agency of the International Convention of the Christian Church (Disciples of Christ). Dr. Bader helped to found the N.E.A. in 1920 and served as director-emeritus at the time of his death.

The N.E.A. provides the indispensable program thrust of preaching, addresses, and fellowship before each Assembly of the International Convention. It has as one of its aims: "To aid in the creation and distribution of literature that will foster in an ennobling way the cause of New Testament evangelism."

Thus far this book is the most ambitious attempt of the N.E.A. in the field of literature. The addresses, given at the

1964 meeting of the Association, were of such high quality and the demands so great that the executive committee agreed that they should be published.

Dr. Edwin T. Dahlberg's sermon, "The Urgent Harvest," was the first of three he delivered at the meetings held in Windsor, Ontario, October 1-2, 1964. It is printed in the closing pages of this memorial volume as a climax and a challenge. One of Dr. Bader's last acts of assistance to the program committee of the N.E.A., was to secure the consent of this great preacher to be guest lecturer for the Windsor sessions. None who heard Dr. Dahlberg's messages will soon forget them.

The five other lectures published herein were given by vigorous, dynamic professors in seminaries of the Christian Church (Disciples of Christ). Each was assigned a definite area of Christian experience and asked to give his best thought to it. These five addresses deal with fundamental facets of the kind of evangelism that not only Christian Churches must master and use, but are basic for the evangelistic witness of other denominations.

These messages express in a real way the deep concern and commitment that Dr. Bader maintained all through his life. Nothing would be a more fitting tribute to him than the assurance that his own brotherhood is continuing to pioneer in new forms and scenes of evangelistic witnessing, undergirded with a solid biblical theological foundation. These lectures speak to the modern mind and will stir the hearts of all who read them.

None who heard or read will soon forget Dr. Bader's statement: "Evangelism is not the only business of the church but it is the church's first business and what Jesus

Christ made primary his church dare not make secondary."[1]
Nor will any who knew him forget his boundless optimism,
his genial friendship, his organizational ability, his search
for new leadership and new ways to bring the good news
of the gospel to those who should commit their lives to
Christ, his Church, and his cause. In a real sense, the Christian Church (Disciples of Christ) appreciates Dr. Bader's
contribution to this basic area of the Church's life.

It all began with a boy who in his early youth committed
his life to Christ. His life was nurtured in a small church
at Bader, Illinois. His undergraduate studies were at the
University of Kansas. He received his theological education
in the Divinity School of Drake University. He was ordained
to the Christian ministry in 1911.

He served First Christian Church, Atchison, Kansas,
where his evangelistic zeal took root and spread through the
entire community, resulting in unusual growth in that congregation. His next pastorate was at Jackson Avenue Christian Church, Kansas City, Missouri. There, too, his capacity
to win people to Christ was demonstrated. He reported
that one of his greatest achievements during his years of
ministry in local churches was the addition of a new member to the church each day.

In 1920 he became the first secretary of evangelism of the
newly formed United Christian Missionary Society of Disciples of Christ. He began at once to hold evangelistic institutes in strategic places across the United States and
Canada. These helped to rekindle the evangelistic zeal of
both ministers and churches.

---

[1]Jesse M. Bader, *Evangelism in a Changing America* (St. Louis: Bethany Press, 1957), p. 13.

In 1932 he was chosen secretary of evangelism by the Federal Council of Churches, later to become the National Council of the Churches of Christ in the U.S.A. He served in this important post until his retirement in 1953.

From the time of his retirement until his death on August 19, 1963, he never lost his deep concern for evangelism. He gave over fifty years of dedicated service to Christ, his Church, and his cause.

The generosity of members of the National Evangelistic Association and a liberal contribution by the Department of Evangelism of The United Christian Missionary Society have made it possible for a complimentary copy of this volume to be sent to each minister of the Christian Church (Disciples of Christ). After this initial distribution, copies may be purchased at one dollar each.

We are indebted to J. Edward Moseley, editorial associate of the Department of Evangelism, for preparing this volume for publication. We are also grateful to The Bethany Press for publishing the book and to Darrell K. Wolfe, director, for valuable assistance in making this project possible.

*Donald M. Salmon,* EXECUTIVE SECRETARY
Department of Evangelism,
The United Christian Missionary Society

*Indianapolis, Indiana*
*January 1, 1965*

# I

# God Reconciling the World
# Through Worship

*Glory to God in highest heaven,*
*And on earth his peace for men on whom his favour rests.*—Luke 2:14.

*From first to last this has been the work of God. He has reconciled us men*
*to himself through Christ, and he has enlisted us in this service of recon-*
*ciliation.*—2 Cor. 5:18.[1]

## RONALD E. OSBORN

Never let anyone force you
to apologize for the vocabulary of our faith. On this point,
as on some others, we Christians have become too defensive.
Now and again some wiseacre accuses us of using language
unknown beyond the stained glass windows, and all too
often we unthinkingly plead guilty. It is time to stop such
nonsense. Both the charge and the confession are false. Our
faith declares, "God so loved the world" and the vocabulary

NOTE: Ronald E. Osborn is dean of Christian Theological Seminary in Indianapolis, Indiana.

[1]From *The New English Bible, New Testament*, © The Delegates of the Oxford University Press and The Syndics of the Cambridge University Press, 1961. These quotations, and all additional Scripture used in this lecture are reprinted by permission.

of our faith is the language of the world—that language used with a daring seldom found elsewhere.

Consider the words of Jesus. Everyone knows what he was talking about when he spoke of salt and light and leaven, of seed and soil and flowers in the field, of birds and sheep and dogs, of buried treasure and a pearl beyond price, of weddings and funerals, of a bare cupboard, of a wandering boy come back home.

But the language of Paul, someone protests, is another story. Is it really? We may agree with the brother in New Testament times who wrote that his letters "contain some obscure passages" (2 Pet. 3:16). Yet there is no doubt about his gospel, and the language he uses comes from man's experience in the world. Cut the apology for a moment and reflect on the great words in his vocabulary. They were not thought up in church; they came from life where it is lived.

*Adoption.* For many a person the word calls up the tenderest recollections of family love and joy.

*Redemption.* It is a businessman's word, from the market in bonds—or from the pawnshop. And in Paul's day it had an even greater intensity of meaning drawn from the slave market.

*Justification.* Change it to *acquittal,* which you find in Weymouth's Translation, and it is the hope of every prisoner who goes on trial for his life.

*Salvation.* The Latinized noun we use only seldom, but nothing thrills us more than the action in the verb—a drowning man saved at sea, a child saved by a miracle drug, a ball game and perhaps a pennant saved by a spectacular play, a marriage saved by repentance and mutual forgiveness.

*Reconciliation.* This, too, is such a word, and we shall examine it more closely.

None of these words is strange. They are all pictures from the secular world. If men do not know what to make of them when we use them in church, the problem is not in the words. The really stunning thought is the gospel which these words declare. In the experience of the New Testament writers, God had entered so fully into their lives that they had to speak of it in analogues from the affairs of every day.

Let us get our point clear. Anyone who hears us preach knows the meaning of redemption; he may not know that God redeems. Every person in the world knows the meaning of salvation; he may not know that Christ is mighty to save. If we have any problem in the church, it is not that our vocabulary is unknown to the world; more likely it is that we have forgotten the three-dimensional worldly impact of the words we use. In our spiritual lassitude we have let them become pale abstractions, ghostly headings in a catechetical outline. The New Testament uses them as joyful declarations of the transforming love of God and men's real difficulty is not in grasping the words but the message, the good news that God is love.

I

Consider then this word *reconcile.* It pictures to us God's action in a world of sixes and sevens.

Every bookkeeper knows the meaning of *reconcile,* every accountant, every weary clerk at the end of the day trying to get his cash register tape to come out even with his sales tickets. The other evening I stopped at a confectioner's to buy my wife a box of candy. The clerk was in no mood to wait on me. She was fussing with her cash and her register tape and muttering, "I'm a penny short." With one red cent I could have reconciled that situation. It cost God far, far more to reconcile the world.

An auditor, we hope, reconciles our financial report or our tax return with our books. Things come out right, an even tally. Reconciliation had much the same meaning in New Testament times. It meant an exchange of money, perhaps from two different currencies, which came out even.

A lawyer, a detective, a judge, a juryman, must seek to reconcile the accounts of a disputed incident, accounts which seem to conflict. A good historian undertakes to reconcile all the evidence pertaining to a particular event. To reconcile is to bring into agreement, to work things out right.

Is this all the word means to us? Not at all. When there is a dispute between two persons, we hope to reconcile the antagonists. Between estranged friends, or partners in business, or husband and wife, reconciliation means joy and victory and hope for the future.

Or here is a person dealt a cruel blow. An athlete is crippled, a child is blinded, a wife is betrayed, a husband is bereaved. In the shock that follows, out of unexpected blackness, he cries, "I cannot reconcile myself to this!" His friends watch helplessly, they surround him with concern, they pray. Then one day, slowly or suddenly, out of his agony, he sings once more and goes on in hope. He is reconciled. Within his heart, though it is still tender, things are set right.

Now we are close to the nub of our problem. It is not in knowing what the word means. It is in suffering so many situations in which there is no reconciliation. We spend our lives in a world where things are not right. Think of all the mixed-up people you know—teen-agers who have not yet found out who they really are, adults who have never fully accepted themselves, all sorts of persons who need "to straighten up the mess that's inside." Perhaps they have even tried and do not know how.

Among the persons with whom we daily work, how many lines of tension there are, how many gulfs of estrangement. With casual acquaintances, such a situation is annoying, with friends it is embittering, with our relatives it is tragic. Beyond our immediate circles, the hostilities are fiercer—bitter and aimless and selfish juveniles living by theft and violence, street gangs cutting and burning, white men bombing Negro churches, black men rioting, proper citizens resorting to economic power and legal subterfuge to keep an evil situation unchanged. The nations are like a parched forest after a summer's drought: the fire may burst out anywhere.

Our best human efforts to reconcile such situations so often result in failure. The boy for whom we get a job fails to show up for work; he robs again to get money for narcotics. The voices of demagogues, white or black, stir up more response than the counsels of reasonable men. A statesman like the late Senator Arthur H. Vandenberg

17

(1884-1951) sits through endless sessions trying to nego-
tiate an agreeement with men who do not want to agree.
The commander of a United Nations truce team in Congo
or Cyprus finds no readiness for conciliation anywhere and
fears being shot at from both sides. Hamlet's cry is not an
isolated outburst of despair, but an analysis of our human
situation:

> The time is out of joint: O cursed spite,
> That ever I was born to set it right![2]

To set things right, to rectify what won't come right—that
is reconciliation. And we cannot manage it ourselves.

Now hear the glad witness of the apostle:

> God was in Christ reconciling the world to himself.
> 2 Cor. 5:19.
> When we were God's enemies, we were reconciled to
> him through the death of his Son.—Rom. 5:10.
> This was his purpose, to reconcile the two [Gentiles
> and Jews] in a single body to God through the cross,
> on which he killed the enmity.—Eph. 2:16.
> Through him God chose to reconcile the whole uni-
> verse to himself, making peace through the shedding of
> his blood upon the cross—to reconcile all things,
> whether on earth or in heaven, through him alone.—
> Col. 1:20.
> From first to last this has been the work of God. He
> has reconciled us men to himself through Christ, and
> has enlisted us in this service of reconciliation.—2 Cor.
> 5:18.

---

[2]Shakespeare's *Tragedy of Hamlet.*

These are the great passages of the God who has set things right. They sing out of lives made right with God, right with themselves, right with their fellow men. And the words are not really hard to understand. It is the experience which leaves man breathless and baffled—unless he has met God on the human scene, until he has known God in Jesus Christ. In the world of nature, so much is out of joint. Within the realm of grace, we are given to see it all set right. And where do we find the realm of grace? How are we enabled to know this reconciling God? In the company of his people who meet him in worship he makes himself known to us, himself and his reconciling work. The God who was in Christ reconciles the world through worship.

## II

Ponder now upon Christian *worship* as our knowledge of the reconciling God.

We are not discussing cultic practices—sacrifices, processions, magic rituals—designed to appease an offended deity. We are not speaking of flattering the King of heaven, as though the Almighty's head could be turned by fawning words of mortal praise. Nor are we thinking of a corporate exercise in self-improvement, a little quiet time apart from the cares of everyday, when men drug their pain with the narcotic of religious sentiment and tell themselves that now they feel a little better to take on the world once more. No, we mean worship in its full biblical sense, worship in spirit and in truth.

Christian worship is communion between God and his people. It is a holy hour of mutual recognition, when he makes himself known to us once more, and we are known of him. It is dialogue between Infinity and finitude, the confrontation of Creator and his creatures, the meeting of Redeemer and redeemed. It is the joyful reunion of the Saviour bidding, "Come unto me," and of his people crying, "Even so, come, O Lord."

In the deepest moments of our lives, we know this kind of experience in our human contacts. Consider the wonder of human love, the way of a man with a maid. The language of lovers sounds like hopeless extravagance. Yet the lovers do not consider their speech overwrought. Quite the contrary. The poor words which we summon up to convey our joy in knowing and being known by our beloved cannot begin to express the fulness in our hearts. Yet this frail bridge of language carries the traffic of love, freighted as it is with thoughts too deep for words. And the lovers understand and are content.

Such communion between two human beings may appear as infinitesimal in the cosmic scheme as the dance of the electrons within an atom. Then look at the stars in their courses. By some such leap from the least to the greatest, from microcosm to macrocosm, we must think of the worship of God. In Christian worship his self-disclosure is celebrated by his people. And we respond in the only appropriate language we know: "Praise and glory and wisdom, thanksgiving and honour, power and might, be to our God for ever and ever! Amen" (Rev. 7:12).

Praise is not the flattery of God. It is our acknowledgment of his glory. It is the most exalted human speech, lisping and stammering to declare a wonder we have apprehended and cannot put into words. It is heartfelt utterance not about something but to Someone. It leads to the confession of our own sinfulness and frailty, but in his grace we know the assurance of acceptance, pardon, and renewal. In knowing him and being known, we are set right.

"Peace on earth, and mercy mild;
God and sinners reconciled."[3]

As we greet him in praise and commune with him in prayer, God accomplishes within us once more the grace of reconciliation.

This is no otherworldly spirituality of which we speak. God's reconciling work through worship takes place in the real world of flesh and blood just as his work in Jesus Christ occurred on the stage of human history. For Christian worship is not mystical flight from the reality of this life; it is earthly declaration, in word and sacrament, of the saving grace of God.

We read the word of Scripture, a testimony to the words and deeds of the Man God sent among us. In the reading we recall and we confront anew the generosity of our Lord Jesus Christ: he was rich, yet for our sake he became poor, so that through his poverty we might become rich (Cf. II Cor. 8:9). We hear the word of preaching. And through this fallible word of a mortal man, the God of our ancient fathers confronts the children of this generation. Only the Lord knows what a feeble instrument our preaching is much of the time, so often ill prepared, insensitive to the questions our people are asking, falling far short of their needs and of his glory. Yet only he knows fully, as we are sometimes

---

[3]From the Advent and Nativity hymn, "Hark! The Herald Angels Sing."

given a glimmering of knowledge, how Sunday after Sunday through the weakness of this spoken word he comes down to confront men in the pew. Lives that have been out of sorts are rearranged. Things are set right. Men are reconciled to their God.

So he meets us in the sacraments and makes things right. The beauty of baptism caught me anew one day under the burning sun as the sand swirled across the Palestinian desert. Weariness, sweat, dirt, thirst—this is the lot of man in that ancient land, with parched lips, and blackened skin, and grit even in his teeth from the blowing sand. Plunge such a man beneath the waters, and he is clean again, cool, refreshed, made new. Here is a powerful witness of the most elemental sort to the way God sets things right with a man.

But not with a man only. With all men. So Paul saw a reconciled humanity being formed by the grace of God—no longer Jew nor Gentile, slave nor free—but all baptized by one Spirit into one Body. So William Stringfellow reminded the 1963 World Conference on Faith and Order that the gravest conflict in our society, the problem of race, is not a social issue at all. It is a question of faith and order. In worship God has already reconciled us through the sacrament of baptism. He has set things right by making of the two one new man.

Or take the other sacrament, Holy Communion. Never can we partake of it, however listless our spirits may be, without a fresh reminder of the supreme act of our reconciliation, Christ's dying upon the cross. "This is my body, which is given for you" (Luke 22:19). "This is my blood of the covenant, shed for many" (Mark 14:24). Here the whole gospel comes to focus, as is indicated in the unison prayer provided in the liturgy of the Church of South India: "Thy death, O Lord, we commemorate, thy resurrection we confess, and thy second coming we await. Glory be to thee, O Christ."[4]

Is it any wonder that Christian worship traditionally concludes with a benediction, an ascription of praise to God and a pronouncement of peace upon his people? For those who have met him in the high hour of worship go forth in the serenity of the reconciled. The linking of these two thoughts is already present in the ancient anthem,

> Glory to God in highest heaven,
> And on earth his peace for men on whom his favour rests—Luke 2:14.

### III

The object of God's reconciliation is the entire *world* of creation. And Christian worship, the meeting of God with his people, points toward that end. It is not intended as an experience of spiritual bliss for the chosen few. Rather, as God meets his people in worship, he is at work to reconcile the world.

The worship of God's people becomes a testimony to the world concerning his great reconciling act. It takes nothing away from the importance of personal evangelism to remind ourselves that public worship is a powerful corporate witness by the people of God to his deeds in Jesus Christ.

[4]The Church of South India, *The Book of Common Worship* as authorized by the Synod of 1962 (New York: Oxford University Press, 1963), p. 16. Reprinted by permission.

Narrating how Paul and Silas sang hymns in the Philippian jail, the author of Acts adds, "And the other prisoners were listening" (Acts 16:26).

In our free, pluralistic society, scarcely a Sunday passes in our churches of any size without the presence of persons from beyond the Christian fellowship. The whole act of worship is a witness to God's deed in Christ. How I wish that such persons could hear our seminarians singing, two hundred strong, in our chapel at Christian Theological Seminary, rather than the restless, tuneless congregations they sometimes wander among. In a generation now past, the church bells proclaimed to people in village and countryside that God and his people were about to meet in sacred fellowship. And still over the din of city traffic there sometimes floats the melody of a well-loved hymn, chimed from some unseen church tower, to remind men of God in Christ.

As a testimony to the world, the cycle of the Christian year speaks the old, old story. How much of the joy and color of our common life, even at the secular level, derives from the great seasons of the gospel, especially Christmas and Easter. Have you read how in recent years Christmas has become a major festival even in Japan, with lighted trees and reindeer? We can decry such celebration if we will, and most of us do, perhaps rightly at times. But can it be that even a secularized Christmas with its tradition of good cheer, of concern for others, of giving, may be used of God as at least a partial means of setting things right in this frantic, troubled world? And is not our real duty as Christians the opportunity of telling all men the true source of the joy we know at Christmas or at Easter rather than

3 8701

denouncing them for their partial knowledge? God's reconciliation is for the whole world, not just for the church.

As God's people worship, then, he makes clear to us his
intention for the whole world. The entire cosmos has been
reconciled through the cross of Christ, not just ourselves.
So in worship we must bring the concerns of the entire
world, not just our little churchly enterprises, before the
altar of God. So often in our devotions we pray to be
delivered from the concerns of everyday, from thoughts of
the world. This is misguided prayer. God does not want
to meet us apart from the real concerns of our lives, but
in the thick of them.

This the architects of the new Coventry Cathedral have
clearly seen. The windows of the church are so arranged
that as the worshipers advance to the altar to receive Holy
Communion they see stained glass, with the imagery of
religious symbolism and their thoughts are turned to the
sacrifice of Christ. But as they return from the Table, they
look through clear glass. There is the churchyard: and beyond it are the smoking chimneys of their industrial city and
all the concerns of their common life—the world of home
and factory and shop and school. So it ought to be with every
church, that we cannot get away from the world, that its
concerns are constantly on our hearts and in our inter-
cessions, that the intentions we form in communion with
God should have to do with the ministry of putting things
right where man live and labor and play beyond the stained
glass windows.

Vachel Lindsay saw the vision of a transformed Congo,
and all of us in our worship should see our world made
over after the will of God:

Lincoln Christian College

'Twas a land transfigured, 'twas a new creation.
Oh, a singing wind swept the negro nation. . . .

Redeemed were the forests, the beasts, and the men.[5]

Our worship then becomes what it was in the New
Testament, the service of God in the world. For his people
walk in communion with him not only in the hour of corporate praise and prayer, but also in the weeklong venture
of labor and witness and service. How many of our Lord's
own parables make this point. The man who really kept
the commandment of God was not the priest, not the
Levite, hastening to the Temple, but the Good Samaritan
who stopped by the wounded man in the ditch and who
set things right.

Or there is that hard admonition in the Sermon on the
Mount: "If, when you are bringing your gift to the altar,
you suddenly remember that your brother has a grievance
against you, leave your gift where it is before the altar.
First go and make your peace with your brother" (Matt.
5:23, 24). Now Jesus did not speak that word to empty our
churches, though it would do so, completely and utterly, if
we followed it to the letter. But he spoke it to put the right
focus on our worship. The real indication that God has set
things right with us will be our concern to make things
right with our fellows in our daily walk. If he has reconciled us, he has also enlisted us in the ministry of reconciliation.

In worship God makes himself known, and more: his
purpose for the world. Worship thus becomes a linking of

[5]Reprinted with permission of The Macmillan Company, from *Collected Poems* by
Vachel Lindsay. Copyright 1914 The Macmillan Company, Renewed 1942 by Elizabeth
C. Lindsay.

the times—the past, especially the historic events of our redemption, and the future triumph of the divine purpose, both caught up in the living present. The great biblical passages concerning the hereafter are not self-centered songs about me and my wings and my harp; they are significant pageants of a reconciled humanity, of a world set right in joy and righteousness and love. And God's worshiping people see such visions not only as prophecy but as mandate. In them is made known his purpose for this world now. Remember the old hymn, sung for many centuries, "Jerusalem the golden, With milk and honey blest"? Under the symbols of biblical allusion, the people of God sing of the final reconciliation, when in the realization of his purpose all shall have been set right.

The call to worship is not a bid to live in the biblical past nor to daydream of the heavenly future. It is an invitation to commune with the God who made himself known in our human history long ago and whose triumph at the end of history will complete his reconciling work. And if through worship we are brought to peace with God, he will lead us to a life of self-giving service, to setting things right in the world of every day.

The English poet William Blake saw it clearly. The Incarnation brought the Lord Christ into this very earthly life which we know. And we to whom in worship God imparts the assurance of his final victory are called to set things right where we are.

> And did those feet in ancient time
> Walk upon England's mountains green?
> And was the Holy Lamb of God
> On England's pleasant pastures green?

27

And did the countenance divine
Shine forth upon our clouded hills?
And was Jerusalem builded here
Among these dark satanic mills?

Bring me my bow of burning gold!
Bring me my arrows of desire!
Bring me my spear! O clouds, unfold!
Bring me my chariot of fire!

I will not cease from mental fight,
Nor shall my sword sleep in my hand.
Till we have built Jerusalem
In England's green and pleasant land.

"From first to last this has been the work of God. He has reconciled us men to himself through Christ, and he has enlisted us in this service of reconciliation. . . . in Christ's name, we implore you, be reconciled to God!" (2 Cor. 5:18-20).

## II

# God Reconciling the World Through Teaching

## JOHN THOMPSON

IN VIEW OF THE THINGS I HAVE isolated that need to be said about God reconciling the world through teaching, I find it impossible to use a text in anything like the usual way. I will try to make this clear as I conclude.

Two men went up to the church to pray. One man was dressed in his "Hart, Shaffner and Marx" suit . . . and wore his expensive clothes with an air of importance as he strode up to the very front pew. Glancing around to make sure his prayerful stance was not overlooked, he prayed,

---

NOTE: John Thompson is Associate Professor of Applied Christianity at Drake University Divinity School, Des Moines, Iowa.

"I thank you, O God, that I am not like other men are. I thank you I am a man of means, for I give to orphanages and old folks' homes. I gave half the money for this very church. People know that I am an *important* man for I belong to all the *good* clubs. I even came to Sunday school as a boy and come to church even today. I thank you that I am not as other men."

The man in the back of the church then fell to his knees and bowing his head cried out, "Have mercy on me, a sinner, O God, for I was *that* man's teacher!"

The haunting meaning of this parable (Cf. Luke 18:10-14) came to be quite forcibly when recently a real estate agent, an active member of a large Christian Church in the community, told me of one of my neighbors who was once a client of his. He had showed him several houses. But instead of making an offer on the house in which he and his wife were interested, he waited until the listing expired and then purchased it directly from the owner thus saving the six per cent real estate commission. The young real estate agent happened to know the boss of this man; he told him what this employee of his had done. The employer assured the agent that he would see to it that this man never received a promotion as long as he was in his territory.

What shocked me in all this was the lack of the spirit of reconciliation—of love and forgiveness—in the attitude of this young real estate man who was a deacon in his church. When he was wronged he sought to retaliate and, in describing this experience, apparently saw nothing amiss in his conduct. He had been reared in the church and exposed to the different opportunities for Christian education at the various age levels. Actually the Christian education program of this congregation is far above average.

Why, after being exposed to Christian education from the cradle roll through the adult departments, were not the basic attitudes of this young man more Christian? Why is not the teaching of the church more effective? Why is it that so many persons are unchanged Sunday after Sunday although they share in the Christian education experience of the church? How is it that "summer is passed and we are not saved"?

Although the church frequently excuses its ineffectiveness because of the limited time for education each week, the real problem is not so much the *lack* of teaching as the wrong kind of teaching. In much of what passes as Christian teaching today, *God is not acting* and it utterly fails to communicate the message of his reconciling love. Such teaching is not Christian, but is, in fact, a taking of God's name in vain. And, a more devastating and damning swearing than that of using God's name when cursing, is using his name when presumably doing good, but failing to go *far* enough and *deep* enough for it to become good *really*.

I

Teaching needs to be creative rather than conforming. One of the reasons why teaching called Christian is so-called in vain is that the teacher presumes there is a fixed content, an elaborated set of sure beliefs to be passed on. Teachers, therefore, endeavor to indoctrinate learners and commit them to certain dogmas. To the degree that teachers are successful in doing this, they merely insure the *obsolescence* of the learners. They turn the learners into pillars of salt. Such teaching is *conforming* rather than creative. Orthodoxy is its patron saint.

Such an approach to education tends to destroy the creativity of the person. There is a "wildness" about man's imagination of which the church seems to be afraid. All too often the education of the church does not allow for the expression of this "wild" quality but expresses it in the interest of orthodoxy and conformity. Teachers of orthodoxy resist new ideas that do not always fit into their neat little pattern. Instead of awakening life to its great potential, it leaves life in a stupor. A being who was created to mount to perfection—to lofty heights—is tragically grounded, only the shadow of a person he might have been. Is not this what the poet, Kenneth Kaufman, describes in the lines entitled "Tame Duck"?

> There are three tame ducks in our back yard,
> Dabbling in mud and trying hard
> To get their share and maybe more
> Of the overflowing barnyard store;
> Satisfied with the task they're at
> Of eating and sleeping and getting fat.
> But, whenever the free wild ducks go by,
> In a long line streaming down the sky,
> They cock a quizzical eye
> And flap their wings and try to fly.
> I think my soul is a tame old duck
> Dabbling around in a barnyard muck,
> Fat and lazy with useless wings.
> But sometimes when the North wind sings
> And the wild ones hurtle overhead,
> It remembers something lost and dead

And cocks a wary, bewildered eye
And makes a feeble attempt to fly.
It's fairly content with the state it's in,
But it isn't the duck it might have been.[1]

When through our teaching a person is less alive when we get through with him, less alert, less sensitive, less human, less responsive, and, hence, less responsible, wherein is the new life which Jesus promises to the believer?

A further example of teaching that dehumanizes the person through a subtle conforming to a certain institutional pattern rather than transforming or creating anew by God's power, is that camouflaged as evangelism but is actually subversive to the gospel and the church. This teaching tends to insulate the person from God and the hearing of his living Word. This is tragically illustrated by a church where forty-seven persons had been received into the membership. At the dinner to welcome them each person was asked to state briefly why he had become a member.

It was reported that the pastor of the church did not commit suicide after hearing their testimonies although it would have been an appropriate conclusion for the meeting. For the answers given to the question, although not original, were much more candid than expected and were much more uniform, disquieting, and discouraging than would have been anticipated.

There were those who answered: "We are new in the community and the fellowship of the church is a good way to get acquainted." And, "We enjoy the sermons of the

[1]Kenneth Kaufman, "Tame Duck," in *Level Land* (Dallas: The Kaleidograph Press). Used by permission.

pastor." And, "Our children like the Sunday school."

But not one of the forty-seven testimonies gave even a hint that a person had united with the church as his or her response to God in Christ in order to become a part of the mission and ministry of Jesus Christ in the world. In fact, the name of "Jesus Christ" was not even mentioned in the course of the forty-seven statements! We hope that it would be different in "our" church, but would it be?

## II

The alternative to teaching that turns learners into pillars of salt is a teaching that encourages persons to be *living responders* to the Almighty's living Word. It is a teaching that is *"enabling"* in that it points the way, but does not get in the way. It takes seriously the scriptural dictum: "Prepare ye the way of the Lord. Make the crooked places straight; get the roads ready for the coming of the Changer. . . . Old things are passed away, in him *all* things have become new."

The need for a Christian education that encourages such openness to God is noted in the story of two men who were living in a houseboat tied to a dock along the waterfront. One night while the men were sleeping, the houseboat broke loose and drifted out into the ocean. In the morning one of the men arose early and went out on deck and began to panic when he saw no land. He called to his companion, "Joe, get up quick. We ain't here no more!"

Are *we* not often tied to the dock of some system of theology or cosmology, or evangelism technique, or institutional structure, failing to comprehend that we "ain't here no more" and that the church must be on the move for here we "have no continuing city"? Only when Christian teachers have the *desire* and have discovered the *means* to be *evokers* rather than *purveyors*—whether this is in the seminary, the church-school class, or the pastor's class—will we develop a Christian education that provides for the *continuous renewal* of man and his institutions.

As teachers, we must not "play God" to our students. There is no more damning blasphemy. Why are we to say by word, by attitude, by implication, "This is the one thing we must do"? Who are we to put our words into God's mind? God is a living being and desires nothing more than to enter into a living relationship with each of his children.

God has many ways of confronting persons and there are many different ways in which persons can *respond* to him and *do* his will. Thus, a teaching that is *"enabling"* in character is a teaching that merely points the way. It acknowledges that the teacher only knows God is wanting to confront the learner. Thus, the learner, through the teacher as God's instrument, is confronted with the living God. The teacher who is faithful to his task must continually confess this *instrumental* nature of his vocation in pointing to God, the Eternal Provoker. Anything less than this, or other than this, is playing God and this teaching is a blasphemous taking of God's name in vain.

It is not the teacher *who* is going to reconcile the world to God, but teaching is the *enabler* through which men and women are able to hear the message of reconciliation. But sometimes, as Christian educators, we begin to think that we have a technique by which the desired result can be secured. No teaching that leaves the impression that *man* by his cleverness is able to reconcile God to man is appropriate to the ministry of reconciliation. As Arnold Come in *Agents of Reconciliation* has so aptly stated this: "It is not the Church's reconciliation, nor is the world to be reconciled to the Church. Nor is it the Church's word and act, as such, that actually reconciles. It is God alone to whom reconciliation and the reconciled world belong."[2]

Thus, the only teaching that is reconciling is the teaching that opens the learner—and keeps him open, alert, alive, and sensitive to the living God who is "in Christ reconciling the world to himself" (2 Cor. 5:19).

## III

With this understanding of our teaching ministry as "enablers," "preparers of the way," "instruments of the Perennial Evoker," we need to consider *another dynamic*. It has to do with the tremendous evidence that little learning occurs apart from involvement.

In much of our Christian education, students and teachers are *spectators* rather than *participators*. Is there not need for local churches and the seminaries to help learners keep intensely aware of the difference between *studying about* and getting *involved in?* Whether our particular launching pad is the local congregation, the state organization, the national agencies, the seminary, or the combination of several of these, we must find means of demonstrating the "getting-involved-in" dynamic.

For example, instead of spending all their time in the church buildings, persons in local congregations who are "learning about" should get out frequently into the world.

---

[2]From *Agents of Reconciliation* by Arnold C. Come. Copyright © 1960, W. L. Jenkins. The Westminster Press. Used by permission.

The Christian Youth Fellowship, for instance, may study about civil rights, but the young people ought to get out and become involved with persons who need to be supported in their appeal for civil rights. In the seminary, instead of merely talking *about* pastoral calling in a stuffy classroom, we need to get out and to meet people in the context of their real predicament.

The church cannot be used by God as his "agency of reconciliation" as long as its "agents" see their ministry merely as attendance at worship, discussing the Bible in a cozy church parlor, serving with committees, paying toward the underwriting of the annual budget—as being involved in "in-church" activities—as important as some of these may be in themselves. Little reconciliation can take place when Christians seek to fulfill their Christian responsibility by merely giving their tithe seated in a cushioned pew in an air-conditioned sanctuary. No church can teach reconciliation and persist in the handling of life with gloves on or at "long distance."

This need for the church's message to be authenticated by *responsible* involvement is illustrated by William Stringfellow's experience of being interrupted by a telephone call. This happened one morning while he was busy in his office trying to get things done so he could catch a plane to keep a speaking engagement. The call was from a pastor friend who served in New York City. The minister told of a widow in his congregation who was going to be evicted because she had been unable to pay her rent. Evidently he thought that Stringfellow, a lawyer, could do something to stave off the eviction so he asked what they should do.

Stringfellow thought for a moment and remembered that

this congregation had some very expensive drapes in its fellowship hall. So he said to his minister friend: "Sell your drapes and pay the widow's rent."

Later, as Stringfellow traveled to the airport in a taxi, he thought back over this incident. He reasoned that maybe he had been too hard on his friend and thought that if there were time at the airport, he would phone him and apologize. But, on second thought, he reasoned, he only told this preacher to do what the church should always do—*become involved at the point of man's need.*

The importance of this dynamic of involvement to effective teaching is underlined by Reuel Howe in these words:

> . . . we should change the *purpose* of our teaching from that of transmitting knowledge *about* the faith to training men for action *in* the faith. People should know the gospel, not for the sake of *possessing* that knowledge, but in order that they may *live* it. The gospel is a saving event that occurs in human relations and is not a body of knowledge for mere verbal transmission . . . Our Lord did not add much to our knowledge of God . . . He embodied God for us so that we could *know* him, instead of knowing *about* him.[3]

We do not mean to minimize the importance of knowledge—it is important. There is nothing more ludicrous than an ignorant ministry, but information is sterile when it is merely disseminated without incarnation in the personal. Our participation in the world's reconciliation, therefore, must be no less concrete than is God's—God is "in Christ reconciling the world."

---

[3]Reuel Howe, *The Miracle of Dialogue* (Greenwich, Conn.: The Seabury Press, 1963), p. 149. Reprinted by permission.

# IV

A further dynamic in the perspective that we are suggesting for Christian teaching is that teaching must be reconciliation rather than mere communication. Although the problem of communication is receiving much attention today, there is a deeper problem. It is that the church's *preoccupation with the problem of communication* may be an attempt to avoid the deeper dimensions of the problem. The problem, as it is frequently posed, is, "How do we make the gospel relevant to contemporary man?"

When it is put this way, we are asking the wrong question. For the gospel *is* relevant, for it is the good news of the living God present in the human predicament in the greatest way that he can possibly be, in the person of his *only* Son. But we are irrelevant as instruments of communication. Our problem is not making the gospel relevant. Rather, the question is, "Am I, as a teacher, relevant to the gospel?" Or, "Is the church relevant to the gospel?"

Even in seminary there is an attempt to evade the real issue, for from seminary we sometimes get the impression that to be more effective in communicating the gospel we must be more theological. So we learn a more sophisticated theological vocabulary, but it is jargon; or we need to be more of a psychologist, so we learn various psychological insights and techniques and, then, we are able to manipulate people.

Although a thorough grounding in both theology and psychology is imperative to an effective ministry, the emphasis here sometimes becomes a substitute for our real need—obedience to the Word of God. It is the word of reconciliation *spoken in a segregated context* that has a hollow sound to it—that is so void of life and hence has no relevance. It is the word speaking of life and resurrection and new being but that has the stench of death—the smell of orthodoxy or conformity about it that is blasphemy. Our irrelevance, you see, is in our standing afar off—we want to keep God at a safe distance, at an arm's length, or, better still, a heaven's distance away.

Therefore, to say that teaching must be relevant is to say that it must be a living Word. To be a living Word, we as instruments must be open, aware, responsive, obedient to him who is the Word. Our words come alive, not just by studying the dictionary to improve our vocabulary, or trying to catch on to this generation's theological clichés, or the latest Christian education lingo, as important as some of these may be, but through *authentic relationship.* For our words to be living, we must be in living relationship with him who is the Word. This does not come through the pride of orthodoxy that says, "I have the Word. You had better listen to me,"or through the security of an evangelism that has learned all the pat answers of the manual, but it comes through a humble obedience in placing yourself beneath the Word as *servant* of that Word.

The authority of Jesus' teaching was of an authentic relationship with his Father and his fellowman. We read of him, he grew "in favor with God and man" (Luke 2:52). He was involved; he participated in the life of God and the life of man to the utmost. It was out of the depths of such relationship that he could say without the slightest trace of egotism or hypocrisy, "The *words* that I have spoken to you are spirit and life" (John 6:63). You see what we have thought to be primarily a problem of semantics is actually a problem in relationships. For to be able to speak a living word is to live in dialogue—in authentic relationship—with God and man.

This authentic relationship *is* reconciliation, and communication is the celebration of this experience. It is the *koinonia* spoken of in the New Testament—man sharing with fellowman the love and forgiveness of God's reconciling love in Christ. Its natural celebration is the communion of the bread and wine for it is only because God was in Christ that it is possible. Furthermore, it is here that comunication gives way to communion and Word becomes flesh and the feast of remembrance becomes the feast of incarnation, and man becomes God's reconciler in Christ's stead. For God's identification with man frees man for identification with his fellowman. Then no longer are there black or white, male or female, but we are all one in Christ Jesus. Reconciliation is no longer just a word but an experience of living in loving relationship with God and man. It is communicating at the level of meaning. The level of meaning is always Truth—not as *proposition,* but as *authentic relationship.* And so, even as Jesus proclaims, life's greatest truth is love—God reconciling the world.

At the *level* of *meaning* you discover yourself a person whose mission in life is to respond to this God who is living, therefore, ever brand new. This means that you have to respond with risks—following the way where Jesus pointed —knowing that way is uncharted for you since *yours* is a *unique potential.* The Master Teacher has shown us only the direction. This is part of the risk we have to take in our living moment, thus that we be charismatic figures—that we be Jesus in his stead—actually daring to do the work he did—a reconciling work—to *be* what he was—*Love.*

Do you see now why these four dynamics—teaching that is *creative, enabling, participating, reconciling*—are important, if not imperative, if we are to be agents of reconciliation in our unique opportunity?

Too, I hope that you comprehend now why it is impossible to take a text for this message—because the Scripture out of which the text for this sermon should be drawn is yet to be written—and can only be written if I, and you and you and you—write it.

As noted, if you have a living God rather than a static pillar of salt, you have also a living Word, for the Word and God are synonymous. If you have a living Word, you cannot have a once-for-all fixed Scripture. What we have in the Bible is the witness of others through whom in the past revelation has been given—insight has come—who in the past have gotten to the level of meaning.

A living God and a living Word require an *alive* response, which means that, over and beyond the use of the witness of the past, there is a witness that must be created in the present. And the use of history must lead to a writing of the Scripture of the present. As God and Amos, in relation, produced a witness, for Amos *hearing* the call of the living God *responded* in the uniqueness of his *potential,* and at least part of the record of that encounter is with us to this day. So, God and Isaiah, in relation, produced a witness. God spoke in a critical hour of Israel's history, "Whom shall I send, and who will go for us?" The young man, Isaiah, said, "Here I am! send me" (Isa. 6:8). God and I in relation must produce a witness—a witness to my seminary students—to my co-workers—to my family—to my neighbors—to my friends—yes, and to my enemies.

So must *you dare* to make a witness—to *be* God's witness —to let go into the record of history the Word God demands *you* make of yourself. More than just reading Scripture, you must *be* Scripture. "You are ministers of reconciliation," reminds our text. Beyond *telling* others of the work *Jesus* did, we must *do greater* work than Jesus did, which God now demands of us. So, it is out of the Scripture *being* written and yet *to be* written by me and all of you that the *text must be chosen.*

Therefore, to our tasks as teacher or learner, for we are always both, may we bring the daring faith expressed in these lines:

> Away, O soul! Hoist instantly the anchor!
> Cut the hawsers—haul out—shake out every
>    sail!
> Have we not stood here like trees in the
>    ground long enough?
> Have we not grovell'd here long enough,
>    eating and drinking like mere brutes?
> Have we not darkened and daz'd ourselves
>    with books long enough?
>
> Sail forth—steer for the deep water only,
> Reckless, O soul, exploring, I with thee and
>    thou with me,
> For we are bound whither mariner has not
>    yet dared to go,
> And we will risk the ship, ourselves and all.

O my brave soul!

O farther, farther sail!

O daring joy, but safe! Are they not all the
   seas of God?

O farther, farther, sail![4]

---
[4]"The Sea of Faith," by Walt Whitman.

# III

# God Reconciling the World Through Preaching

## RICHARD C. WHITE

Modern America is ripe for the plucking, but preaching seems unable to reap the harvest. The figure of speech is, you will remember, one which Jesus used. It is appropriate to our subject. Modern America is ripe for the plucking, but preaching seems unable to reap the harvest.

Reconciliation means estrangement ended, separation ended, guilt and remorse absolved, emptiness and alienation defeated by fulfillment and identification. Modern America is ready and anxiously awaiting such a message.

NOTE: Richard C. White is Professor of Homiletics at Lexington Theological Seminary (The College of the Bible), Lexington, Kentucky.

There are many signs of estrangement and emptiness and alienation to be seen in the corporate and individual life of our nation.

The man in the gray flannel suit is not so sold on money and position as he seems to be. He is restless, threatened, fearful. Even as he spiels the "party line" and plays the expected role to get his promotion, he knows the boss has ulcers along with his salary and status—and he, himself, is already feeling a rumbling in his midsection. He does not really like the scramble.

The defiant teenager recklessly challenging authority is not enjoying himself as much as he seems to be. He is searching for an authority and a value system which promises him more integrity and identity than he sees in his elders. He is reaching, looking, longing, however, belligerently.

Neither the militant integrationist nor the hard-core racist is as sure as he seems that his philosophy is a real panacea. Each is only grasping after a little piece of reality as he defines it. There seems so little else that is secure, dependable, in a world which appears to have left him out in the cold, cut off from life.

The modern multiplication of the means of utilizing leisure time does not mean that people really enjoy all the tenting, boating, traveling, and "do-it-yourselfing" which is going on. Rather, it may be only a frantic search for a new diversion to help obliterate the disappointment of the last one tried.

Perhaps people stand by and watch a woman slowly murdered with good reason—there is no reason in them for doing anything else. I believe they are appalled at the lack.

Whatever else may be true of us, modern America is cut off from nearly all of its old loyalties and directions and inner motivation, alienated by indifferent social structures, and threatened with loss of identity. It hurts, and the hurt is voiced, if only we will listen.

America is ripe for the plucking, but much of our preaching is not doing any reconciling because it is not addressing the situation.

Some preaching fails because we do not recognize sin when we see it. It has modern costumes. We are often fooled by the comfortable, affluent façade of modern life and assume that people in church only need "bettering" while people outside the church are not interested. Both of these ideas are dead wrong. But we won't see that until we see *modern* separation from God in its modern dress.

Some of our preaching fails because we are tied to outdated, irrelevant approaches and methods. Many honest listeners, if candid, would respond to much of our preaching, "I just don't dig you, Dad. You're like squaresville." It's time we recognized that the theological language of the eighteenth and nineteenth centuries is a dead language, understood only in theological seminaries, and their outposts—the pastors' libraries.

Then some of our preaching fails because we have lost faith in the power of God to work in preaching. The simple fact is that many of us preach many sermons and expect nothing to happen because we have preached. Since the people, also, do not expect anything to happen, it does not. Our founding fathers berated Roman Catholics for telling beads and rattling off prayers. A lot of our preaching must seem just about as useless and formal as they felt those activities to be.

Furthermore, some of our preaching fails because we only address the symptoms of sin and do not get at the disease. We are good at denouncing alcoholism, divorce, delinquency, immorality, but not so good at addressing the real evils which drive weakened people into such things. To say it another way, we can make the guilty and the desperate even more remorseful and despairing by denouncing their behavior, but we cannot help them understand their compulsions and lead them to a more magnificent obsession.

I

To preach reconciliation today demands a current tactic of approach. It is not yet clear in all details just what the tactic is, but three things do seem obvious.

One, we must find points of contact with man's awareness of his emptiness, inhumanity, fear, and frustration. Some beatnik poetry speaks more directly to such estrangement from God than does most preaching. Some modern literature and drama (even with its lurid lewdness) touches the aching void of desperation and depersonalization in man far better than much of our traditional preaching. We must discover how and why and learn new points of contact.

Two, we must show that God's reconciliation redeems from *modern* alienation and estrangement. It *does* cure ulcers and provide identity and meaning and self-respect. It *does* make time worth using, so you do not have to find new ways of wasting it in diversion. But those facts are not obvious in the traditional preachments. We must show that

God's antidote *works* on modern illnesses.

Three, we won't do any such preaching of reconciliation unless we really believe it is possible. If preaching is not an exhilarating opportunity to be used by God really to accomplish deep changes in people's lives, then it is only a worthless ritual—a time-consuming bother to the preacher who already has too many things to do—and a dull bore to the people. Reconciliation assumes that people are estranged, and they are. It also assumes that God has done something about it, and he has, but we are not getting that message to the people.

To be plucked by the Lord of the harvest and garnered into the sheaves to be saved *still* means being uprooted, but we may be unwilling to accept that fact. The New Testament words for reconciliation mean "to change," "to make other," and they are intensified by a prefix which means "completely" or "thoroughly." The first century Christians heard this passage say, "In Christ, God was completely changing us toward himself." Note that it is we who are changed. "Reconciliation" is too easy a word. It does not really say which side is giving in to the other, or whether both give in a little. To be reconciled to God means to be made thoroughly other, to be changed throughout.

The ancient Hebrews sought reconciliation by attempting to change God's disapproval to approbation and acceptance. The Old Testament backgrounds of the word mean "to cover—to overlay—to besmear or paint." Thus they often mean to make oneself acceptable and attractive to God by covering one's ugliness and defilement. A person, or a thing (like the Ark or the Temple) could become defiled. God was obviously displeased so an offering was made to satisfy

God's anger and righteousness and earn his favor. Reconciliation often meant changing God's displeasure to approval by offering or sacrifice.

This idea has one thing in its favor. It acknowledges that our sin cuts us off from God, turns his face against us, makes us guilty and anguished. The Hebrew was quick to recognize his defilement, his separation from God; and he wanted to do something about it. But he wanted God's anger to change, not his own basic nature.

There is still much such activity in our preaching and worship today.

## II

Too much of our preaching expects little or no real change in the person. It too easily assumes that Christ has appeased God's wrath and made us acceptable in our sinfulness, *because* of the sacrifice. All you need to do is to believe that it is so—Jesus has done all the suffering that is necessary to appease God's righteous anger at our sins.

Too often we pray for forgiveness and forbearance, asking *God* to be moved by our supplication. "Give ear, O Shepherd of Israel. Hold not our sins against us. Stay your wrath and show us your favor." It is as if our prayer would change a vengeful God into a loving and forgiving Father.

There is too much easy salvation offered. "Only believe. Come down and say yes and God will take care of you and do the rest." Or, on the other hand, "You were reared in a Christian home; you're already basically Christian, just be good and everything will be fine. God has made it so." Either of these ways is too easy and unbiblical and unreal.

Most astute listeners know somehow that anything as deep and pervasive and painful as their aimless "lostness" cannot be so easily answered.

To preach reconciliation is to proclaim that God changes man and that God needs no change, that he is already gracious and loving. Preaching proclaims that God has *changed* man, not just accepted him as he is. We proclaim that the man who hears and heeds the Word is never again the same man, but a new and different man, part of a new fellowship which nurtures his newness and continues to change and redeem him for God's purposes. In Christ we *are* changed because we are shown that God seeks us out *anywhere,* even on Wall Street or Madison Avenue. We are changed because we are shown that he is not a vengeful judge whose anger can be appeased by our petty action. Rather, he is a father who has sired children to belong to him, and who will not leave them nameless and wandering orphans in a hostile world. Instead, he reaches out even into the pig-pens and draws them back with his love. And when they know that, they will leave the pig-pen and their profligate ways and idolatrous self-importance and *be* changed.

Perhaps it is time we stopped preaching, "Join the church and God will be on our side" and started preaching, "God has jerked the rug out from under our twenty-five dollar Bass moccasins and stood us on our heads in front of a mirror and thus made new men of us." Perhaps it's time we stopped praying, "O Lord, show us thy favor," and started praying, "O Lord, what now? I see I'm a new man. Now, what do I do first?"

All the Old Testament and much of the New Testament usage of the word reconciliation involves sacrifice, bloodshed, death. Jesus is pictured in this context. The implication is clear—reconciliation is costly. It cost God the life of his Son and it does not come cheaply and easily to us. Let us not just give middle-class respectability to man's littleness and anxious, ulcerous "lostness" by preaching an easy salvation which leaves the basic personality unchallenged and unchanged. The Philippian jailor said, after Paul had preached, "What must I do?" There was desperation in his voice. How often have we heard that at the door of the church after our sermons? Reconciliation means *we* are changed, not God.

### III

Though we are given a ministry of reconciliation, we must never forget that God is the Lord of the harvest. Paul says we are ministers of reconciliation. I have been saying much about what we do, but the great danger is always that we will overemphasize what we do. It is *God* who does the reconciling.

The ancient Hebrews' idea of reconciliation never realized this. One Old Testament idea was that a man could reconcile God's anger by making his own sacrificial offering which would be pleasing to God. Another idea did develop the notion that the priest could make an offering for one estranged and that made the offering more efficacious to change God's anger. But they never really grasped the idea that *God changed man's sinfulness,* only that God used man for his purposes. When man was sinful, he had to effect the reconciliation by his or the priest's action.

Much modern churchly activity repeats this error, in practice if not in theory or theology. Our understanding of the

Bible can assume that the words and ideas recorded there, when spoken by a human voice, are the power of reconciliation. But this may be bibliolatry—words on paper are not God's Word—nor is the human pronunciation of them —God's Word is God's action.

Remember that passage which says that *God* added daily to the church those who were being saved? Let us not look for God in the words of the Bible and make of those words another sacrifice to be offered up to him when spoken by some modern priest. Our understanding of preaching itself can lead us astray here. In our enthusiasm, we may overemphasize the importance of our role as preachers. I would be the last to say we should throw out homiletics and skillful use of all our personal abilities in preaching. I hope though I would also be the last even to imply that the power of human rhetoric and personal persuasion ever reconciled anyone to God.

There is an insidious temptation in the zeal to preach, to be an agent of reconciliation. It is illustrated by the story of the evangelist of another day who told that wherever he found himself (on a train or visiting with strangers), he always asked himself, "Which one here is the one God wants me to win?"—wants *me* to win! The same thing is seen in the slogan often used in evangelistic lay effort— "Each one win one"—as if *we* were really doing the winning.

Concern for the lost wherever we are—willingness to witness to our faith—YES! But any deep-hidden suspicion that *we* are God's gift to the unsaved sinner—NO!

Again, our methods of evangelism can get in the way of God's reconciling action. We can become stuck in outdated approaches and patterns, because *we like* them, we are experienced in them, we feel at home with them, we do them well. We must always remember, God moves in history—and history moves because God is in it. Speaking in tongues has passed from our particular scene. Perhaps some other things should also. Our campaigns and strategies may be used by God, but they may also get in his way!

Paul said preaching was foolishness to lots of people; and the way we do it, it sometimes is, because we think we can command the spirit by our mechanics. But the spirit bloweth where it listeth.

The world is ripe and the message can garner a harvest if it is relevant and understood. We are agents of the reconciliation the Lord of the harvest proclaims, but remember: it is not we who speak, but God who is at work in us. "Thanks be to God for his unspeakable gift" (2 Cor. 9:15). Amen.

# IV

# God Reconciling the World
# Through Personal Witness

*So we are ambassadors for Christ, God making his appeal through us. We beseech you on behalf of Christ, be reconciled to God.*—2 Cor. 5:20.

## J. DANIEL JOYCE

$\text{I}$T IS A SIGNIFICANT OBSERVA-
tion that is made by Dr. Gene Bartlett in his book, *The Audacity of Preaching,* that we stand at least one person away from the full possession of most of life's deepest realities. It stirs me deeply when I understand that God has left a "person gap" between me and most of life's greatest and deepest realities. Dr. Bartlett enumerates several of these realities and I appreciate the fact that he has called these to our attention, even though most of us knew this to be the truth already.

NOTE: J. Daniel Joyce is Dean of The Graduate Seminary, Phillips University, Enid, Oklahoma.

We shall not love until someone has loved us first. The psychologist and the pastoral counselors know well that we are not able to love until we have been loved. There are *great resources* in this world for the healing of humanity, but there must be a physician to stand between those immense resources and the one who is to be healed and relate the resources to need.

There is the greatest body of knowledge now available in the world that has ever existed. In fact it is phenomenally greater than at any other time in the history of the world, but there are millions who live in ignorance because it requires a teacher to relate that knowledge to uninstructed minds.

God has graciously granted to us the disclosure of himself with all his loving kindness and tender mercy to be known by men, but there stands the "person gap" which someone must step into and fill before that grace and mercy can redeem our lives. The distance between our need and the resources of God which are near to us is indeed a tremendous hiatus. The distance between the God who reconciles and the one who seeks him is a terrific distance and only a person as a witness can fill that gap. Just as it is necessary for a parent to mediate God's love to a child, so also it is necessary for a witness to mediate God's love to man.

The priesthood of all believers has come to mean something a little different to this generation than to the generation of the reformers. It was then interpreted to mean that all men had access to God through Jesus Christ and every man could be his own priest with Christ as the high priest. It connotes something different to us today, almost a paradoxical and contradictory fact; i.e., that all men need some person to be their priest in the critical as well as the usual situations of life. Everyone needs a priest to represent the love, mercy, and forgiveness of God, to complete the triangle of fellowship in which God and neighbor are the other two partners. This is to say that the mediation of God's reconciliation and his grace awaits the witness of his people in the most personal relationship of life.

What does this mean for your life and mine as personal witnesses? What does it demand, to measure up to the opportunity which God has given us?

There are lots of tricks in the evangelistic bags of Christendom today. There are many techniques offered, some good and some not so good. There are all the powers of modern communication and transportation at the command of the evangelist, but these in themselves will not answer the question. There are many opportunities for the techniques of mass psychology, group dynamics, and the manipulation of the masses of people, but something more is required of us than any of these to fill the "person gap." I should like to pursue this demand. Let us consider the man in the gap.

I

To mediate reconciliation demands a genuine and authentic person as Christ revealed the dimensions of a person.

Nothing else can bring about the reconciliation which God has provided because that reconciliation is extremely personal. Reconciliation is a special image in Paul and a personal one. This is the characteristic interpretation of the salvation work of Christ. It is dominant in the writings of

57

Paul and he is more explicit than any other New Testament writer to tell us what reconciliation really means.

It is the picture of two persons finding each other and sharing each other's life after being alienated. It is more personal than justification as we have studied it in the theology of the Reformation. It is more than restoration of something previously known, a return to some kind of status quo. It is a moment of exhilaration and incomparable joy in finding one who has been lost from you or estranged from you.

A man acquitted before a judge is not as significant an image as the father running to meet the prodigal in the way and falling on his neck to kiss him—God putting himself at man's disposal. In the book of Philemon, the word "reconciliation" is not used at all, but the concept is so explicit. Dr. Amos Wilder pointed this out in a speech in Montreal.

The story reads like the story of the Prodigal Son, when Paul seeks to reconcile Philemon and his slave. Love is the context and Paul makes his appeal on the basis of love. He calls upon Philemon to receive back the slave as "a Christian brother" and not to receive him back in the same status in which he had been. He calls upon Philemon to recognize the newness of Christ which belongs to a slave as well as to a master. God had used Paul in the "person gap" and God's reconciliation had been mediated to a slave. And then, the witness puts his own life on the line to effect the reconciliation with Philemon. He calls upon him to receive the slave as he would receive Paul himself. He places his own name and reputation and work in jeopardy to effect the reconciliation of Onesimus and Philemon because *God* has received Onesimus as a son.

In the sixth chapter of 2 Corinthians, following our theme passage on reconciliation which appears in chapter five, there is another statement from Paul which delineates the personal nature of this reconciliation. He calls upon the Corinthians to receive him and God's mercies by "widening their hearts." Since the theme of reconciliation is the last part of chapter five, it is also the context of chapter six. These two passages throw light on each other, one of them speaking about reconciling man to man and the other speaking about reconciling man to God. In both cases, reconciliation means "widen your hearts."

The personal nature of this special image of Paul is abundantly evident in these passages and he himself was great enough, genuine enough, and big enough to be God's person in the "person gap." I hope we can measure up to the opportunity when and where God gives it, and be trusted with the intimacies of life and the mysteries of God's grace to fill the gap as genuine persons belonging to God.

## II

To mediate reconciliation demands a willingness to share life at the point of its deepest meaning.

This is to say that it demands a priesthood. To fill the "person gap" demands of us not alone speech, not alone mind, not alone heart, not alone work, not alone skill, but all of these which means that we share our very selves or souls. Could it be phrased better than has been done by Paul when he said to the Thessalonians, "So, being affectionately desirous of you, we were ready to share with you not only the gospel of God but also our own selves, because you had become very dear to us" (1 Thess. 2:8). The meaning is that "We yearned for you and longed for you to belong to the family of Christ; we wanted you so much for him that we were ready not only to speak or to work or to fellowship with you, but we were ready to share our very souls [and this is a literal translation of the word *pseuchas*], because you had become so dear to us in Christ."

I recently heard a football coach recounting what he had said to his team at the mid point of the game. He said, "Men, you cannot win this game at arm's length. You cannot do this with your hands alone because football is a body-contact sport." This sport was conceived as a body-contact sport. There is no way to play the game without being drawn into a man-to-man and body-to-body relationship.

So it is with evangelism. There is no way to play this "game" at arm's length or by staying aloof from those whom we would lead to Christ. This is a soul-sharing and soul-searching game. To fill the gap which God has left demands of us the person-to-person, heart-to-heart, and soul-to-soul relationship. Jacques-Benigne Bossuet, the great French preacher, has said that it takes more faith and courage to speak one or two words, face-to-face, with just one person, than it does to preach from the pulpit to two or three thousand listeners.

It demands a sharing of life at its deepest meaning, which is the sharing of faith, of hopes, of ambitions, and of love. The most effective plan for our work is God's plan that the whole body of Christ shall be a priesthood which shall pour out its life into other lives and seek to permeate the whole lump. In no other way can the hiatus be filled or the chasm be bridged than by a personal witness.

It does not require a lawyer, nor a debater, nor a person skilled in the art of rhetoric. An evangelist is not necessarily any of these. He is one who testifies, exhorts, proclaims, and witnesses to the reconciliation which God has already granted to us. In essence, he is a *koinwnos,* a sharer, a fellowshiper, one who divides himself with others. That is why Paul says in our passage that we are ambassadors on behalf of Christ as though God were making his appeal through us. The entreaty of God must be seen somehow in the life of the witness, or the gap will never be filled. God wants to see men reconciled because he himself has already granted their forgiveness, but they must know it and confirm it and confess it and receive it.

The priesthood of all believers would truly mean that every one of us is a priest who is called to mediate this reconciliation to every man on earth. The saving grace and love and work of Christ is to be mediated to the people through priests and we are God's priesthood.

### III

To mediate reconciliation demands an unusual love.

I am struck with Paul's statement that they were ready to share their souls because Paul had become "so dear" to them. The people whom he sought to win in Thessalonica had become so beloved, so dear, that unusual things had begun to happen. There is a strong word here in the original text which seeks to convey the yearning on the part of the man who was standing in the gap.

Something stronger than the usual has to manifest itself on the part of the church or our evangelistic gains will be meager. We cannot continue to operate with the same kind of love we have demonstrated and hope to achieve any great results.

It was not many years ago when a speaker before one of the gatherings of the National Council of Churches said that the church must get its life off the line of mediocrity or expect to cease to have any impact on the character of American life. We must get off dead center. This could not be more true than it is in our situation in regard to evangelism.

Our passion for the lost does not now go beyond the bounds of mediocrity, as far as I am able to tell. There is no evidence of a precedent-shattering love directed toward those who do not have communion with God. A mediocre program of any kind is not good enough for the present day. A mediocre love, least of all, is not good enough to make any impression on the world or turn anybody's face toward the church to hear a message of redemption.

When we read John 3:16, we say that the word "so" is the biggest two-letter word in the New Testament. For God "so" loved the world that he gave his only Son. But the word "so" in this statement from Paul also has tremendous meaning and is one of the biggest short words in the New Testament. The phrase "so dear" is used in the New English Bible and in the older American or Goodspeed Translation.

I can speak about orphan children and the pathos of their plight and this will stir mightily your emotions and bring tears to your eyes perhaps. This is because these children have no parents and no family. Can we in the same way speak about persons who are alienated from God and who know not the divine love of the family of God and produce the same kind of mighty emotional stirring? There are many around us who have no communion with God through Christ. Remember the words from the old gospel song?

> Down in the human heart, crushed by the tempter,
> feelings lie buried that grace can restore.
> Touched by a loving heart, wakened by kindness
> chords that were broken will vibrate once more.[1]

We must speak about and demonstrate the unspeakable, indescribable, incomparable love of God. Christ said to us, "the hairs of your head are all numbered" (Matt. 10:30, Luke 12:7). I do not know how fully what it means but I get the message in its central focus, namely, he loves you with an unspeakable love. I think I love my wife and my four-year-old son, but I have not thought of expressing it in such a way as this. This language speaks about the magnitude of God's love which is almost beyond our comprehension. At its very least, it means a love that goes beyond all bounds of the usual or the mediocre and kicks the perimeters off our regimented and stalemated lives.

A great Christian of the Congo once said that he was only "ten per cent converted" when he started working to help convert others. Bringing other people to Christ aided him, in turn, to become more than a "ten-per-cent Christian." Only this kind of love can fill the gap.

## IV

To mediate reconciliation demands an ambassadorial consciousness.

---

[1]From the song, "Rescue the Perishing."

We are ambassadors on behalf of Christ. In the actual opportunity, this means that the handling of the situation by the ambassador may draw men to Christ or may drive men from him. We are ambassadors as though God were entreating through us. This leaves us no other choice than to urge men and persuade men to be reconciled to God.

The ambassador transmits the yearning of God for the lost, to the lost. He testifies, as one whose life is at stake, in the outcome of the trial, on behalf of God. He tells men that God has already forgiven them in Christ and that he has not dealt with them according to their sins nor counted their trespasses against them. He tries to awaken them to God's merciful offer, to treat them as righteous people even though they are not. He feels the hand of God upon him and he testifies as one who is sent. "I sat alone, because thy hand was upon me" (Jer. 15:17). When life responds with some consciousness that God's hand is upon it, effectively mediating the reconciliation of God will not prove difficult. "All this is from God, who through Christ reconciled us to himself and *gave us* the ministry of reconciliation" (2 Cor. 5:18).

We have a word which is not ours and we belong not to ourselves but to him who has created, preserved, and redeemed us. This consciousness produces the true freedom which is spoken about so often in writings of our New Testament. We shall know the truth and the truth shall make us free. Is it not paradoxical to say that the ambassadorial consciousness of belonging to one another produces our true freedom? Nehru once said that you may be free when "willing to give up voluntarily anything that can be taken from you."

We are not our own. We have been bought with a price, a fantastic price. Then the greatest fact of our Christian existence is that we belong. Dietrich Bonhoeffer found comfort in this fact during the last lonely and trying days of his struggle on earth. To confess this, brought him strength and inspiration. He wrote:

Who am I? They often tell me
I stepped from my cell's confinement
Calmly, cheerfully, firmly,
Like a squire from his country house.

. . . . . . . . . . . . . . . . . . .

Who am I? They also tell me
I bore the days of misfortune
Equably, smilingly, proudly,
Like one accustomed to win.

. . . . . . . . . . . . . . . . . . .

Who am I? This or the other?
Am I one person to-day and to-morrow another?
Am I both at once? A hypocrite before others,
And before myself a contemptibly woebegone weakling?
Or is something within me still like a beaten army,
Fleeing in disorder from victory already achieved?

Who am I? They mock me, these lonely questions of mine.
Whoever I am, Thou knowest, O God, I am Thine![2]

This text tells us plainly who we are. We are ambassadors on behalf of Christ as though God were entreating through us.

[2]Dietrich Bonhoeffer, *Prisoner for God, Letters and Papers from Prison* (New York: The Macmillan Co., 1953), p. 165. *Letters and Papers from Prison* (London: Student Christian Movement Press).

I think to stand in God's "person gap" and measure up to the demands which that situation makes upon us, will require all that we have said here and more. None of us will feel that he has been successful and none will have reason to glory, except in the fact that God has placed him here. But the more we become personal witnesses and see the salvation which God will mediate through us, the more we shall know that high honor of our calling, to stand between the Creator and his creation, to stand between the healing and the sick, to stand between the revelation of God and the wandering sheep, being a *person* through whom the creation is perfected.

The whole creation groans in travail, waiting for the full redemption of the sons of God. It seems that we can even hear the muted cry of the birds and beasts and trees of the field for the perfection of God's creation which only awaits the reconciliation of mankind to him. We believe that all the world will be won to Christ and this is a part of the scandal of our faith. It is really not the question whether or not you are able to stand in the gap, but rather, "Are you willing?"

# V

# God Reconciling the World Through the Church in the World

*All this is from God, who through Christ reconciled us to himself and gave us the ministry of reconciliation; that is, God was in Christ reconciling the world to himself, not counting their trespasses against them, and entrusting to us the message of reconciliation. So we are ambassadors for Christ, God making his appeal through us. We beseech you on behalf of Christ, be reconciled to God.—2 Cor. 5:18-20.*

## WILLIAM D. HALL

THE MESSAGE IS TWOFOLD: (1) God *has* reconciled the world to himself, and (2) we must be reconciled and become ambassadors of reconciliation. The two seem to be contradictory. We have been reconciled; therefore, we are commanded to be reconciled.

The seeming paradox is clarified by a study of the meaning of the parable of the Prodigal Son (Luke 15:11-32). The son produced the alienation by his own rebellion against the father. The father does not need to be reconciled because he was never alienated. It was the action of

---

NOTE: William D. Hall is Associate Professor of Missions at Brite Divinity School, Texas Christian University, Fort Worth, Texas.

the son which brought the alienation. But the alienation could not be ended until the son "came to himself," re-established his life in its true center, returned humbly to his father's house to ask forgiveness for his rebellion. He did not deserve the acceptance which he received. On the basis of his "just deserts" he deserved only the rejection, the hostility which the elder brother gave him. We are reminded "that while we were yet sinners Christ died for us." So, without deserving it, he found himself accepted and living in the household of faith.

The story does not end there. The reconciliation had taken place; he was living in his father's house. Yet he had to be reconciled again and again. Habits of speech and thought from life in the far country would find expression, and words would slip out which brought an expression of pain to his father's face. Such actions and thoughts are not worthy of one living in the father's house. So, not once, but every day, he had to fall at his father's feet and say, "Father, forgive me. I have sinned before heaven and in your sight."

This is the nature of the reconciliation which God effected in Jesus Christ. We have been accepted. We do not live in an alienated world where God is remote and where we have to earn our way into his fellowship. The greatest saint could never earn his way into the household of faith. We live in a reconciled world where God has accepted us, unworthy as we are—"while we were yet sinners." Still we must be reconciled. Not in order to earn the place in the household which God has freely given us, but out of gratitude for his grace, we must be reconciled, we must live the good life. There is all the difference in the world between living the good life in order to earn salvation and doing it out of gratitude for salvation which has been received through God's grace, not through our merits.

The difference between these two views of religion is illustrated by the Buddhist version of the Prodigal Son. In the *Lotus of Perfect Law,* the son leaves home and spends many years, finally returning in rags and misery. He does not recognize his father, but the father recognizes him and tells his servant to take him to the mansion and to clean him up. Still not revealing his identity, he waits to see if the son will become worthy to become a son. He assigns humble tasks and leads him on through encouragement.

Not until his son had become used to his duty, withstood temptation, and broken himself of a mean spirit did the father reveal his identity. He formally declared him to be his heir, and introduced him to his relatives, the king, and other people.

This father did not accept his son while he was still unworthy. He waited for him to develop a better human nature step by step, giving him some humble and suitable work. The father treated his son according to the stage he had reached.

The one story illustrates the salvation that is earned through righteousness on the basis of works of merit. It accepts the kind of world where man has to earn his position and end the alienation by his own effort. The other illustrates the salvation, but where it is granted freely even while he is unworthy because through faith he is able gratefully to accept God's gift of reconciliation. Christians have seldom grasped fully the vast difference between these two kinds of salvation, and much of our trouble in evangelism stems from this confusion.

## I

The first task of the Christian is to accept the reconciliation which God has given freely in Jesus Christ—to accept it joyfully and thankfully, living a life of faith and righteousness in gratitude for it. With unerring insight our founding fathers placed the emphasis at the right place. They perceived that all the theology a person needs is contained in the question, "Do you believe that Jesus is the Christ, the Son of God?"

If he is not the Christ, then the world is the same kind of hopeless place that the non-Christian religions have believed it to be. Man gets only what he deserves—and who wants to get what he deserves? It is an alienated world in which man has to work his long, weary way up to fellowship with God through great moral achievements, through asceticism and mortifying the flesh, or through the infinite withdrawal which leads to the achievement of great mystical insights. It is the kind of place in which man basically must save himself. God is not really concerned; he sits remote and unattainable in the heavens. Man must devise his own strategies and methods of working out his own salvation.

Some see it as so difficult a process that they feel that many lives will have to be spent in transmigration before a man can achieve the measure of moral perfection which will admit him to fellowship with God. This is a dismal prospect. There is no "good news." There is no "peace." Man is at war with an unfriendly universe. His religious systems and moral principles are a part of the strategy for winning this war by his own efforts. He lives in an alienated world in which the reconciliation which Paul talks about has definitely not taken place.

If Jesus was the Christ, then there is "good news." We are not living in an alienated world. The reconciliation has taken place. There is cause for rejoicing. "God was in Christ reconciling the world to himself." God treats man, not with strict justice, but with grace giving him far more than he deserves—counting his faith for righteousness. Man does not have to earn his place in the household of faith, as the other religions maintain, but he—like the Prodigal Son—has been granted this status freely in spite of his being unworthy. The elder son who had earned his place in the household had rejected it by his own attitude and ended outside the household of the father by his own choice. Such is the contrast between the salvation which is faith through grace, unearned and not capable of being earned, and the salvation by works through the Law, which neither accepts God's gift of reconciliation nor can achieve it by its own efforts.

Those, like Arnold Toynbee, who urge Christians to make common cause with other religions, fail to see that in doing so the Christian would be accepting the view of the other religions which holds that the world is not reconciled but is still alienated. The Christian claims that the alienation is ended, God has once and for all done the deed of reconciliation. He did it in Jesus Christ. This act of God in Christ is precisely what the non-Christian cannot accept. To him the war still goes on. He calls the Christian to join him in working out better strategies for fighting a war which the Christian believes is ended. In the interests of a spirit of good fellowship and cooperation with the other religions, shall we give up our belief in reconciliation? Shall we drop this most basic of all Christian beliefs? For we believe that God has ended the alienation, that in Christ he effected the reconciliation; that the world is a different kind of place as a result—a much more hopeful place than the non-Christian sees it. The non-Christian, and those Christians who question the sending out of missionaries to carry on evangelism, deny that God did any such thing. For them the peace has not been made; for them the war still goes on.

James Stewart in *Thine Is the Kingdom* reports that, "James Denney once heard a distinguished missionary say: 'Some people do not believe in missions. They have no right to believe in missions: they do not believe in Christ.' "[1] Unless one believes the statement in Matthew 28:18, "All authority in heaven and on earth has been given to me," he has no right to "go . . . and make disciples." For a "therefore" connects the two statements.

If Jesus is not the Christ, if all authority was not granted to him, if God was not in him "reconciling the world to himself," then our only authority for evangelism is our own —and this is not enough. Then the Christian can only go out to proclaim that "my religion is better than your religion," or "I am a better person than you are," or "my church is better than your church," or "my culture is better than your culture and I want you to copy it." None of these reasons is good news. In fact they are declarations of war, and other people so interpret them. If our evangelism is by

---

[1]James Stewart, *Thine Is the Kingdom* (New York: Charles Scribner's Sons and Edinburgh, Scotland: The St. Andrew Press), p. 15. Reprinted by permission.

our own efforts and on our own authority, we merely increase the conflicts, the hostility, and alienation in the world. We certainly do not effect reconciliation.

When I hear people say, "Christianity is all right for *us,* but their religion is good enough for *them,*" I wonder if they know what they are saying. If Christianity is false, then it is not good enough for us. We are following an impostor who claimed for himself what was not true. He was not "both Lord and Christ"—in fact, he was not even a very good man. The most we could claim for him is that he was a good teacher whom we admire. But if the claims of our faith are true, they are true for the whole world and not just for *us,* for he is "Lord of Lords and King of Kings." He is Lord of the man on your street who has not accepted his lordship. And he is Lord of the man in Calcutta who has never heard of his lordship. Both men need to be told. And one of the chief responsibilities of Christians is to tell this good news—to evangelize.

If the first disciples had not recorded and told what God did in Jesus Christ, we could never have known of it. Certainly it is not the kind of thing some wise man could dream up for himself. This good news runs counter to that kind of human wisdom. And for the same reason if we do not tell—evangelize—others can never know that "God was in Christ reconciling the world to himself."

Much of the reticence about carrying on evangelism comes from a misunderstanding of what the good news is that we have to tell. In an address I heard Bishop Newbigin mention an encounter in an Indian village when a Hindu stood and challenged the preacher, "You ask us to unite in Jesus Christ, but you Christians are hopelessly divided. You ask us to become Christian, but Christian lands are filled with divorce, crime, and threats of war and destruction."

What answer could a Christian give to such charges? They are true. He could only reply, "I cannot point to myself and my accomplishments. You may well be a better man than I am. I cannot point to my culture, because much of what you say is true. I can only point to my Saviour, who is your Saviour as well as mine. It is him I offer you, and this is all I have to offer—not my goodness, or my religious accomplishments, or even my superior religious system."

Being an evangelist is neither presumptuous nor pretentious. It is a very humbling experience. But obviously no one can approach the task with either assurance or humility unless he truly believes that Jesus is the Christ, the Son of God, that "all authority" was given to him, and that in him truly "God was reconciling the world to himself." There can be no evangelism unless we accept the good news fully and joyfully.

## II

The second phase of our task, according to the Scripture is to see the church, and ourselves as a part of it, as "ambassadors for Christ, God making his appeal through us." Paul was quick to see and to point out that it was not enough to accept God's act of reconciliation. We must also be reconciled to God. We must live lives worthy of those living in the household of faith, not to earn our place in it, but because we have freely been given a place in the household. The task of the Prodigal Son was not over when he had been accepted in the father's house. In gratitude and humility he, day by day, had to be reconciled to his father.

He could not be satisfied with himself as he was, nor could his father be satisfied with him in that condition. He had been accepted, but to go on sinning "so that grace could abound" was to reject the grace which had been so freely granted.

The church, as the Body of Christ, must be the continuing channel of God's grace in the world and must serve as the ambassador of reconciliation. It is not just a hospital for sick Christians, as some would have us believe when they conceive of churchmanship as sitting at home waiting for the preacher to come and call on them. It is "the people of God" who are charged with carrying on God's mission in the world. It can only fulfill this function, the very function for which it was brought into being, if it keeps its life open to the working of the Holy Spirit within it. For God has chosen to carry on his work of reconciliation in the world through this weak and very human organization, the church.

The Hindu denies that God could work through a body of people, a congregation, the church. He is like the man who, passing a gigantic fish mounted on the wall, says, "The man who caught that fish is a liar!" To him there can be no entity such as Christians claim the church to be. He believes that God works only through individuals—not through a congregation. Salvation, for him, is a purely individual experience, with each man gaining his own mystical insights, and working his long hard way to God. Men can get together to share their insights. They can share the insights of the great seers of the past. But the only purpose in getting together in a congregation would be such a sharing of insights. For him, God does not work through groups of people.

The Christian, on the other hand, says, "This is precisely the way God does work. Those who have accepted God's gift of reconciliation band together to live under the influence of his Spirit. They are transformed by the working of the Holy Spirit within them. This is how God's work of reconciliation takes place. The church is the channel of his working."

This view of the church makes for certain problems. The world is apt to say to us, with the philosopher Nietzsche, "Show me that you are redeemed and I will believe in your Redeemer." The people of God in the church must produce the fruits of the working of the Holy Spirit, or their witness will not be acceptable. The lives of Christians must be eloquent evidence of the transforming power of God at work in their midst. If God is making his appeal through us, then our lives will be evidence either of transformation or of stagnation and failure.

Only the church which has been reconciled and is being reconciled and transformed can be a minister of reconciliation. A church can grow without meeting these requirements. It can grow because it tells people what they want to hear, because it confirms men in their beliefs in the standards of society. If it is a one-class church it can serve as a step on the status ladder, as Gibson Winter has pointed out so effectively in *The Suburban Captivity of the Churches*. Such a church may grow, but for the wrong reasons. It may be filled with people who have never accepted God's reconciling act in Jesus Christ but who are busy earning their own salvation through works of merit—not saying "Hail Marys," but by working at church suppers, leading the scout troop, and serving on a functional committee. Such a church cannot be an ambassador of reconciliation because it has not accepted reconciliation in Jesus Christ. When it goes out to get new members it may be a huckster of religion, a salesman of peace of mind, or the promoter of a club which seeks to grow, but it cannot truly carry on evangelism, because it has not accepted the "evangel"—the good news which Christians are called to proclaim.

On the other hand, even small and weak churches can be effective instruments of evangelism. Size and wealth are certainly not the criteria. The reason for the effectiveness of village churches in India is that they are little groups of witnessing Christians banded together as the household of God in that place. They are doing as a congregation what the Hindu says cannot be done, serving as a channel for the working of the Holy Spirit in the community. What is happening before the eyes of their non-Christian neighbors is the transformation of their lives and the life of their community. This is the evangel. They have become Christ's "ambassadors of reconciliation."

Hindus who thoroughly disapprove of the process of conversion and who hate the church and its challenge to what they believe, will say, "This was formerly the dirtiest part of the village; now it is the cleanest. It was the most profane; now it is the only place where you hear no profanity. It was the most dishonest; now these are the only people in the village whose honesty you can really trust. What kind of religion can do this to people?"

I have been called in India to confer with relatives of Christians in a nearby village. When questioned about their interest in the Christian faith, they replied, "We want to know more about their religion. These relatives of ours have been Christian for several years. We don't know what has happened to them, but they are a different kind of people now. Whatever it was that has happened to them, we want it to happen to us." This is how the church carries on its ministry of reconciliation in the world.

## III

There are other ways in which the ministry of reconciliation manifests itself. Christians are called to be the conscience of society, and this is not easy, because we are called to challenge the very values and methods which society holds most dear. We seek to be peacemakers, but we are most often looked on as troublemakers. How many Americans can see Martin Luther King, Jr., as a minister of reconciliation? But this is what he seeks to be. There can be no easy peace with the injustices and inhumanity of our society, and no Christian can live at peace with such things. But true reconciliation can come only when we are willing to accept God's view of the situation rather than our own. This is what the Christian is called to do.

One preacher, who was criticized for preaching things which his congregation did not want to hear, replied, "I know that you don't like to hear what I say. I don't like to hear the kind of thing that I have to preach any more than you do! But I have to preach God's Word, whether it is comforting or disturbing to my human feelings, my selfish interests, my cultural values, or my pet prejudices."

We are called to be witnesses to the reconciliation which God has wrought; not to try to reconcile God's ways to the world's desires or its accepted values. And this responsibility does not make it easier for us to live in the world; it makes it harder. We are promised, "In the world you have tribulation; but be of good cheer, I have overcome the world" (John 16:33). Either we live in a false and misleading peace with the world—the injustices and false values of society—or we accept the real peace which comes only from God and give up the easy-going peace of the world.

Becoming a Christian in India does not bring peace between a man and his Hindu neighbors. It is more apt to bring hatred and persecution. No more is it likely to bring peace in our society. To speak of the Christian world mission as "Christian World Fellowship" is to misunderstand it. Those of you who have John Birch Society members in your churches know that challenging their "culture religion" and their religion of patriotism does not bring peace in the church or in the community.

Jesus said, "Do not think that I have come to bring peace on earth; I have not come to bring peace, but a sword. For I have come to set a man against his father, and a daughter against her mother . . . and a man's foes will be those of his own household" (Matt. 10:34-36). Faith in God, living under the Lordship of Christ and the guidance of the Holy Spirit, tears out of our lives the things we hold most dear. It is a painful process—as much so as if it had been done with a sword. We have been violently wrenched away from the center of our existence, from obsession with ourselves and our own selfish interest. The peace of God that is victorious and which results in true reconciliation because it ends the fears and hostilities that have been shaking our off-center lives to pieces, comes only as we find the true center of all life. When we accept the Lordship of Christ we have re-established balance and poise, because life has been restored to its true center—faith in God. It is only when this has been done that the individual Christian or the community of Christians can speak confidently of the good news.

Occasionally the suggestion is made that the seminary should teach more courses on evangelism. One man even suggested that we have a department of evangelism. This seems to assume that the weakness of the churches in evangelism is in techniques and methods. Churches may not use the best methods available, but our sickness is one of faith and not of techniques. Installing a lot of "how-to-do-it" courses, either in the church or in the seminary, will not cure it. Either the whole life of the church or of the seminary produces the kind of faith and spiritual climate which produces a strong evangelism, or the problem remains insoluble.

There is no system which can be taught that will make the church effective in its ministry of reconciliation if the church has failed to be a channel of reconciliation. One cannot preach effectively what he has not believed. One cannot witness effectively to God's reconciling act in Christ unless his whole life is testimony to that faith.

I know of no way to teach a church member or a seminary student to be an effective channel of the grace which he does not possess. The most skillful teacher or program planner is bound to fail if he is trying to make the unsaved serve as effective channels of God's salvation, trying to get them to be witnesses for a message which they neither accept nor practice. As Cleo Blackburn's mythical Aunt

Cindy puts it: "You can no more give away what you ain't got than you can come back from where you ain't been!"

So we end as we began by confronting ourselves, and all Christians, with the basic question of faith. Do we truly believe that "Jesus is the Christ, the Son of God?" Do we live in a world where reconciliation has taken place, or do we live in an alienated and hostile world? Can we accept as the basic fact of our lives that "God was in Christ reconciling the world to himself . . . and entrusting to us the message of reconciliation"?

# The Urgent Harvest

*Do you not say, "There are yet four months, then comes the harvest"? I tell you, lift up your eyes, and see how the fields are already white for harvest.*—John 4:35.

## EDWIN T. DAHLBERG

T HE WEEK BEFORE THE NEW Delhi Assembly of the World Council of Churches in 1961, Mrs. Dahlberg and I spent a week in Assam, India, where the Baptists of that jungle area were celebrating the 125th anniversary jubilee of our Baptist work in Northeast India.

It was an unforgettable experience. Six thousand delegates—more than half of them young people—had come together from all parts of Assam. Among them were Garos, Nagas, and other hill tribes representing some eighteen different linguistic groups, many of them in ceremonial cos-

NOTE: Edwin T. Dahlberg is Minister-in-Residence at Crozer Theological Seminary, Chester, Pennsylvania.

tumes with shields and spears. Never have I been so deeply moved as when preaching to this throng. Seated on the grassy floor of the vast *pandal*, or tabernacle, made of bamboo and palm leaves, they were divided into twelve language groups, each of them with its own interpreter.

As each speaker came to the rostrum the interpreters would stand in the midst of their respective companies and translate, sentence by sentence, the sermon that was being delivered in the pulpit. This they did with powerful gestures, and voices of passionate intensity, so that the preacher had a feeling of the Holy Spirit's tremendous re-enforcement. It was like Pentecost. What a mighty vindication of the missionary command of our Lord, "Go therefore and make disciples of all nations" (Matt. 28:19).

One of the speakers on that occasion was Dr. John Skoglund, who occupies the Chair of Theology and Missions at the Colgate-Rochester Divinity School. He had come from Calcutta by automobile, with a native driver. The rice harvest everywhere was in full swing, the fields literally and vividly white unto the harvest. As they were going along a certain road, Dr. Skoglund noticed three Indian women out in one of the fields, gathering the grain. With their sickles and their colorful costumes they made a lovely picture, almost biblical in its setting. Like other American tourists, Dr. Skoglund was anxious to get a striking picture to show to friends back home. He asked the driver to inquire of the women whether they would be willing to pose for a picture. Soon the driver came back from his conversation with them, shaking his head. "No," he explained. "They said, 'Can't he see we are busy with the harvest? We have no time for such foolishness.'"

At no time in my life has there been brought home to me so forcefully the urgency of the harvest. The women were right. We have no time for foolishness. We cannot waste our time on things superficial. In the church this is true. We must be busy with the harvest—proclaiming the good news of God in Jesus Christ, winning the souls of men, women, and children to the Kingdom. There is no time for wasted effort—poorly thought out programs, the damaging competition of rival churches and denominational systems, the appeal to personal and ecclesiastical vanities rather than to the Cross of him who died to save us all from sin.

I

The harvest is urgent because of the urgency of the message.

Preaching at a Lenten service in Christ Church Cathedral, St. Louis, on his last visit to America, the late Dr. John Baillie of Scotland held up his Bible and said, "On every page of this Book there is written the message that we are wanted and loved, that God wants us, that God loves us."

What is more imperative than that in our hate-filled, love-starved generation, this message should be lived, demonstrated, and proclaimed? Millions upon millions of people, in our land and in all lands, are living and dying without the slightest consciousness that anyone wants them or loves them, much less the God and Father of our Lord Jesus Christ.

During the Christmas season that followed the New Delhi Assembly, Mrs. Dahlberg and I were visiting our youngest son and his family in Kengtung, Burma. Before the recent expulsion of all foreign doctors by the Burmese government, he served for five years as a medical missionary in the East Shan States. He is now continuing his work in Thailand, just one hundred miles across the border. His assignment in Burma was among the hill tribes, some fifty miles from Red China, where, with the exception of one or two government doctors, he was the only fully trained physician for an area of 250,000 people.

Christmas morning we were visiting the village of Pangwai, some 5,000 feet up in the mountains, where he had an outdoor clinic. This is the mission station where Paul and Elaine Lewis of Denver, Colorado, are doing such a valuable evangelistic work in addition to their translation of the New Testament and the hymn book into the Lahu, Shan, and Akha languages.

It was a beautiful day but more like Easter than Christmas. The cherry blossoms were in full bloom, their delicate pink shades contrasting vividly with the dark green of the pines up and down the mountain side. Thousands of bees were humming in the branches.

That afternoon I was to preach the Christmas sermon at the little Baptist Church of Pangwai. Because it was the only opportunity I had to preach to this remote congregation, I decided to preach on John 3:16, which contains the heart of the Christian message. Knowing that there would be five linguistic groups present—Lahus, Shans, Akhas, Burmese, and a few Chinese—I met with Mr. Lewis and the five interpreters in the morning to find out whether there would be any words in John 3:16 that might be difficult to translate.

"Yes," said Mr. Lewis. "You will have trouble with the

word *world.* These mountain people have no word for world in the same sense that we have. They have a word for *soil,* and a word for *dirt,* but not for a *world of people.* They know little about the rest of Burma. And as for Europe and America, that is beyond their comprehension. You will have to find a way to overcome this."

So I prayed that the Holy Spirit might help me to clarify the meaning of the word *world* for these people who were also loved and wanted by God. The best I could come up with was something like this:

"I live so far from the village of Pangwai that when it is daytime here it is nighttime in my village of St. Louis. But even though our homes are as far apart as the night from the day, God loves my people in the village of St. Louis just as he loves you Lahus, Shans, Akhas, Burmese, and Chinese in the village of Pangwai. In fact, he loves us all so much that he sent his only begotten Son, Jesus Christ, to live and die among us, and for us, so that whoever believes in him should not perish but have everlasting life."

This promise happened to be especially personal to me that day. Just the day preceding, down at my son's station in Kengtung, I had preached to the Lahu congregation on Christmas Sunday morning. Only minutes after I came out from that service, I had been handed a cablegram saying that my last surviving brother, Henry, had died suddenly of a heart attack in Denver, Colorado. He and his wife had been in Kengtung and Pangwai two or three years before our own visit, while engaged in some research as to the possibility of sugar beet culture in the Oriental countries. They were known to some of the members of my congregation in Pangwai.

So I said, "Some of you will remember my brother, Henry, and his wife, Irene. Yesterday I received word that my brother died suddenly last Thursday. This fills my heart with much sorrow. It was this brother that led me to Christ when I was a boy, and I loved him very much. But though I have sorrow today, I do not despair. For I know that through the promise of Christ, God's Son, which I have just read to you, that my brother is at this very moment standing in the presence of our Saviour, in a world far more beautiful even than the world we see here in Pangwai on this lovely Christmas afternoon."

I wish you could have seen how eagerly these mountain people listened to this message. They came for the most part from animist religions, which are religions of great fear—fear of death, fear of darkness, fear of the evil spirits which they believe to be lurking in every stone, tree, and river, ready to leap out at them in the twilight. Nothing gives them such a sense of joy and wonder as the good news that Christ and the prophets of Israel have brought to us, that God wants us and loves us.

We need this faith in America as much as in Burma. We, too, live in fear—fear of war, fear of automation, fear of death, fear of communism, fear of racial strife, fear of all the enmities and perplexities of the Nuclear-Space Age. I am not sure that we have a word for *world* either. Our world, like that of the mountain tribes of the East Shan States, is also a world of *soil* and *dirt*—real estate values, housing developments, water rights, timber rights, mineral rights, oil wells, and airfields. We do not yet comprehend the world of Christ, which is a world of human beings—white, black, red, yellow, and brown—people for whom

Christ died. Nothing is more urgent than the message that God loved the world, and that through repentance and faith in Christ we must be prompt in entering into that love.

## II

The harvest is urgent also because of the urgency of the world situation.

The late Arthur Holly Compton, winner of the Nobel Prize in Physics, and for several years chancellor of Washington University in St. Louis, once brought this out in a telling way. Revealing to a group of friends some of the struggles of conscience he experienced while working on the atomic bomb, he said:

"We must realize that we are no longer living in a world of horse and buggy wars. Our situation today is comparable to what it would be if a father and mother going out for the afternoon should call their little children to them and say, 'Mother and Daddy are going to be gone for an hour or two, and we want you to be good children. Here are some things for you to play with until we come back—a box of firecrackers, a box of skyrockets and Roman candles, some sparklers, a keg of gunpowder, and a box of matches. Now be careful. We'll be back soon.' "

That is precisely the kind of world in which we live.

During the three years I was president of the National Council of Churches I went on Christmas Missions for three years in succession to military installations all over the world —Alaska, Spain, Morocco, Hawaii, Guam, Okinawa, Formosa, the Philippines, and Hong Kong, as well as to the Strategic Air Command Center in the United States, and to the Atomic Energy Center at Oak Ridge, Tennessee. I was appalled by the extent of war preparations everywhere —the stockpile of weapons—the vast areas of the earth devoted to military purposes. The children of God are truly playing with cannon crackers, gunpowder, rockets, and matches.

Not only so, but we are teaching our boys and girls how to carry on this philosophy in the next generation. In a newspaper article, James Smart said, "My annual study of the Sears Roebuck Christmas catalogue has satisfied me that the toymakers of America are continuing to prepare our children for the realities of life in the world around them."[1]

He then pointed out that there were thirteen pages given to war toys, but only one page to Nativity scene figurines. The emphasis today is on jungle fighting and guerrilla warfare. You can even get a jungle-camouflaged bicycle with a toy machine gun. There is a game called "Spy Detector," in which you win by tracking down foreign agents. Another is called "Risk." "Build up armies in strategic spots," the catalogue explains, "to invade continent after continent in a bold plan to conquer the world." But the "best" game of all is called "Time Bomb." One player sets the timer, and tosses the bomb to the next player. He tries to get rid of it before it goes BANG! The player holding the bomb when it goes off is eliminated.

This should cause us to re-examine our whole educational system. Is not the education of our children gradually being taken out of the hands of the church, the home, and the

---

[1]James Smart, "Toys Help Kids for Real Life," *Philadelphia Sunday Bulletin,* Sept. 27, 1964.

school, and taken over by the commercial world, the entertainment world, and the military world?

Our leaders of evangelism and Christian education must take this matter seriously to heart. We have already indoctrinated two whole generations of youth in the most efficient means of death and destruction. Where will all this end in the next generation?

I sometimes marvel at the way people worry about "socialized medicine" and a "socialized economy." What we should really worry about is a militarized medicine and a militarized economy. This is the real threat to free enterprise. Our whole civilization is geared to the production of military hardware. The transfer to a civilian economy is one of the major problems at which we should now be working.

It is time the Christian Church stepped into the picture and took the initiative. Why should we let the Pentagons and the military sciences of the nations "grab the ball" and run down the field with it? The Christian Church is the greatest security council in the world. Its gospel and its mission constitute the supreme hope of mankind. It is only in God that our defense is sure.

You may wonder what all this has to do with evangelism. The answer should be clear. In this kind of a world, we need a new ethical content to our evangelism. All too often we have been preaching in a moral and spiritual vacuum, as if the good news in Christ were some disembodied thing, without any relation to the present dilemma of mankind. We must make it plain that the acceptance of Jesus Christ as Saviour and Lord involves some new and specific forms of repentance, related to such things as economic justice, race relations, war and peace. Yes, and related to the growing vulgarity and violence of our alcoholic culture.

Some people challenge the right of the church to enter into this field. One of the leading laymen of one of our great denominations tried to persuade the General Board of the National Council of Churches a few years ago to abandon all social and economic pronouncements. He wanted it to limit itself to the preaching of the gospel, to missions, to humanitarian service, and to other matters not connected with controversial issues. He did not succeed. He failed because he had a mistaken and inadequate view of what is meant by the whole gospel.

Can we carry out the missionary enterprise as Christ commanded, for example, and make disciples of all nations, while we ignore the issues of world disarmament and the efforts to ban the bomb tests? Millions of dollars' worth of missionary property—hospitals, schools, and evangelistic centers representing the dedicated stewardship of Christians all over the world—have been destroyed by wartime fires and bombing raids. As a result of these same wars and the hatreds and fears generated by them, our Bible teachers, doctors, and missionary workers have been expelled from whole areas of the earth, as in Red China and certain areas of Africa. Where the missionary enterprise has not been set back by wars and rumors of wars, it has been hampered by industrial exploitation, race prejudice, and other forms of apostasy. Shall the church have no voice? Shall it have no right to cry out to mankind, "This must cease"?

*Life* magazine never spoke a truer word than when it said that we have been caught in "the terrible silence of the decent." Unless we speak, as the Bible speaks, we are lost.

For the judgments of the Lord are true and righteous altogether, and they will surely be visited upon us. The harvest is indeed urgent.

III

The harvest is urgent, finally, because of the cry of the human soul for deliverance.

Joseph Fort Newton, the eminent minister, in his autobiography, *River of Years,* said at the close of World War II that "a sob follows the evening sun around the world."

Who is there that has not listened to that sob in the sunset?

My journeyings have followed it around the world. I have heard it in the prisons of many nations. I have sensed it in the tears and the trembling of the alcoholic in his lonely hotel room. I have been shaken by it in the pleadings of teenagers begging that something be done for their fathers and mothers so as to change their minds about getting a divorce. I have been overwhelmed by it in children's wards where I have seen little babies with the skin of their arms and hands and ears nibbled away by rats in their tenement homes. I have been staggered by it in the Church World Service Centers where long lines of homeless and starving refugees waited for one little bowl of rice, or one tiny sweater for a child shivering in the cold.

Must that sob of humanity continue forever? Maybe so. But in the meantime, we cannot escape the words of Jesus when he read,

"The Spirit of the Lord is upon me, because he has anointed me to preach good news to the poor. He has sent me to proclaim release to the captives and recovering of sight to the blind, to set at liberty those who are oppressed, to proclaim the acceptable year of the Lord" (Luke 4:18-19).

The whole human scene was personified for me one afternoon in the psychiatric ward of a great hospital in St. Louis. I had been visiting a man from my congregation who had had a nervous breakdown, but who was soon ready for release. All the time we were talking together, I was conscious of a strange cry from far up at the other end of the corridor. It was repeated, over and over:

". . . SOMEBODY! . . . . . . SOMEBODY! . . . SOME-BODY! . . ."

The patient I was visiting said to me, "Pastor, on your way out would you please stop and see that boy? He is a high-school lad, only sixteen years old. He was just admitted here this morning. He has been calling that way ever since."

Ordinarily I would not visit an emotionally disturbed patient on his first day in the hospital without the permission of the psychiatrist. But as I was passing by the open door of this lad's room, he saw me. Strapped to the bed, he called to me, anxiously,

"Doctor? . . . Sir?"

I paused in the doorway and said, "I am not a doctor. I am a minister."

He repeated his question. "Doctor? Sir? Am I sunk? Am I done for?"

"No," I said, gently. "You are not sunk. You are not done for. For God loves you. He is going to make you well."

As I drew near to his bed, I spoke to him in quiet tones, and asked him if he would bow his head with me in a moment of prayer in God's presence. This he did.

When I left him, he was quiet, at least for the moment. The outcome I do not know.

Ever since that day, from all parts of the earth, I have heard that desperate cry:

". . . SOMEBODY! . . . . . . SOMEBODY! . . . SOMEBODY!"

It is the cry of statesmen, of business and professional men, of young people and children, of homes on the boulevards and homes in the slums, of scientists, soldiers, and ministers, too—a cry like that of the blind man calling from the roadside, "Jesus, Son of David, have mercy on me!" (Luke 18:38).

Are we sunk? Are we done for? NO! The promise is still true, "For God sent the Son into the world, not to condemn the world, but that the world might be saved through him" (John 3:17).

This is the message we are commissioned to proclaim. God forbid that we should be guilty of "the terrible silence of the decent."

269